RUGGER . . . DO IT THIS WAY

SUGDEN   BARLEE   HOLLIS   [*Frontispi*

£350

£350

RUGGER

DO IT THIS WAY

Learn Your Rugger from Photographs

by MARK SUGDEN

Dublin University, Wanderers, Barbarians and Ireland

and GERRY HOLLIS

Oxford University, Sale, Barbarians and English Services

With Photographs by

JOHN BARLEE, F.R.P.S.

JOHN MURRAY, ALBEMARLE STREET, LONDON, W.

First Edition . . 1946

Made and Printed in Great Britain by Butler & Tanner Ltd., Frome and London

FOREWORD

BY D. R. GENT

On New Year's Day, 1925, there appeared as scrum-half for the Irish International side a new player, by name Mark Sugden. The match was against France in Paris. Ireland won by a penalty goal and two tries to a try, and Sugden had had the honour of scoring a try in his first International match. The Selectors were so pleased with their new man that they put him into the side for the " big match " of the year, that against England at Twickenham. Again he played well, as did all the side, for England were very lucky indeed to avoid defeat, the result being a draw of two tries each. In the same side as Sugden were W. E. Crawford, G. V. Stephenson, the brothers Hewitt (T. and F. S.), G. R. Beamish, W. F. Browne, J. D. Clinch and J. C. McVicker, all great names in the history of Irish Rugby.

In the last match of that 1924–5 season, Sugden was given a new partner, E. O'D. Davey. He, too, was a great success on his first appearance and these two kept together from that season till the end of 1930–1 season, making probably the best pair of half-backs that Ireland has ever had. Davey went on a little longer than Sugden and played, in all, 34 games for Ireland as against Sugden's 28.

Well, that is who Mark Sugden is and a finer scrum-half I don't wish to see. He was completely equipped for the job—plucky, agile, splendid at picking up and passing out, a capital tactician, and with quite a touch of genius for knowing when to go on his own. There is one little corner of the Lansdowne Road ground at Dublin that is known as Mark Sugden's corner, for he used to make a practice of scoring there in all the International games and especially against England. He was born in England and was at school at Denstone before returning to Dublin and playing for Trinity, Wanderers, Leinster and then Ireland.

In Gerry Hollis we have a real " modern," one who was watched with admiration in War-time Services Internationals, when he played football of the highest class. I wish the boys who want to learn this great game had seen Hollis going for the line, with men to beat and men to race, chest out, head back, and a powerful hand-off ready as well ; at Murrayfield, Leicester, Gloucester, Richmond and other places. It was just grand. Stockily built, very well developed, resourceful, plucky, he has been a splendid wing three-quarter, who must have played nearly everywhere behind the scrum since his St. Edward's days at Oxford, and then in the Oxford side in 1938, for he is such a handy size. Incidentally, I believe that H. B. Toft, the Waterloo, Lancashire and England forward of

1936-9, was called in for consultation. He was in the England side the season before the War and is what the world calls an " expert hooker," a very sure sign of his modernist tendencies. Suggestions on forward play have been approved by Toft and there has been no more thoughtful forward or one more interested in every aspect of forward play than this witty, wise and skilful Lancastrian.

Well, this is the side that has been responsible for this most excellently produced little book of instruction in Rugby football. This glorious game, glorious mainly because it is so vigorous, is best learnt by trial and error—in the open, a field, a ball, sides, kicking about, passing movements, dribbling, tackling, scrummaging, and so on, all under the eye of someone who knows the laws of the game and has, by actual and prolonged playing, learnt its spirit as well, who will check and correct and (if age permits !) show by example how best to play the game in all its aspects. That method beats all books, blackboards and photographs, and especially if it is supplemented, as it nearly always is, by visits to big matches and the watching of one's heroes. This is a game for hero-worshipping, if ever there was one, and the number of these grand boys and men, who have given their lives for their country in the recent War and other Wars, has provided more support still to the opinion many of us hold—that no game brings out all that is best in men so effectively as Rugby football does.

But this action photograph book should also help tremendously. Here are the main movements of the game performed by two famous players, admirably photographed, with just enough explanation to enable the actions to be copied. Budding players will be fascinated by the photographs—and Barlee has made an excellent job of them— will love learning how to pass or kick or take a ball or tackle as Sugden or Hollis does, and will be bound to improve their game by conscious and unconscious imitation.

One last word. This book has for its background the Royal Naval College, Dartmouth, temporarily domiciled elsewhere, but still our one and only Royal Navy. Great players have come from the Royal Navy—N. A. Wodehouse, E. W. Roberts, W. J. A. Davies, C. A. Kershaw, G. H. D'O. Lyon, W. G. Agnew, W. G. Luddington and K. A. Sellar are just a few of them. Rugby football is an integral part of the life of any Institution, College, School—yes, and even Fleet. In the Inter-Services matches at Twickenham, we love to watch the " sailors " and especially on a wet day when they have an opportunity of showing their traditional prowess at dribbling and tackling. This book is valuable in the great help it will be to learners and teachers of the game : it is more valuable still because of its " place of origin."

D. R. GENT

Spring 1945 (Gloucester and England)

THE BRIGHT IDEA

YES, this is " just another book on Rugger." Many, better qualified than the two of us, have written hundreds of pages on this very subject. But we have our reasons for producing this book, and the book has a definite object.

The autumn of 1944 found us both coaching Rugger at the Royal Naval College, Dartmouth, trying to convince patient Cadets that an ability to run straight or tackle low was the only hope of salvation for potential Naval Officers. Talk of coaching led to a discussion of ways and means, which prompted the conclusion that teaching by eye was infinitely preferable to teaching by ear.—What should a tackler do, exactly, at the moment of impact ? How does a good scrum-half get the ball away so quickly ? Just how does a " hooked " ball come out of a tight-scrum ? Many of us can explain all this in general, but what should it all look like in action ? Many of us can demonstrate a great number of the points, but not all of them. " Photographs " was the obvious answer. Whereupon Barlee pricked up his Irish ears, produced a camera and said : " Why not see what we can do ourselves ? " And this self-challenge was the reason for the appearance of the book.

So much for the idea of the book, but what of its object ? We decided to aim at simplicity in demonstrating the fundamentals of the game, for the benefit of young players themselves and their coaches. There are no records, no reminiscences, little discussion and no diagrams. The book is divided into three parts : Part I being the basic " drills " on which the game is built, Part II comprising more advanced technique, and Part III consisting of " departmental " and team-work.

No doubt well-qualified readers will find obvious omissions. It was difficult to decide what to leave out, but we wanted to avoid delving too deep. Other critics will find faults in the technique shown in the photographs ; we expected that. We have merely demonstrated the methods which we have found effective in playing and coaching. Further, if ever Rugger coaches come to agree on everything, alas, what a dull thing coaching will become and how stereotyped the game ! From a photographic point of view, we must admit and regret the fact that the plates were taken at different times, often in varying rig, which gives the photographs an irregular look. But, whereas we hoped to rattle them all off in an hour or two, we were sobered to find how often re-takes were necessary, until finally the photographs were taken over a period of months.

We must thank the Cadets who came to our aid so cheerfully to help to photograph Part III. We worked them hard all one afternoon and they responded well, despite the heat and the fact that they had not played Rugger for three months previously. Officers and Masters helped nobly with the tight scrummaging. They, too, perspired freely in the heat for, as the buttercups and daisies show, these particular photographs were taken when Summer was well on its way. It is hard to think that after such labours, the only reward of some Officers and Masters is to appear " seat first " in the book !

Three individuals need special mention for their assistance. First, Wren Cato, an M.T. driver, who gave her services in typing the manuscript (between driving trips). The actual typing was simple in itself, but having to interpret Hollis's writing proved a real ordeal. Second, Bert Toft for his helpful vetting of the detail in much of Part III : sage advice, kindly given. Third, Mr. E. A. Hughes, who volunteered to read over the proofs and rectified the more unorthodox forms of English grammar in the text.

On with the book now. Each photographic plate is numbered ; opposite to it, on the printed page, is a short explanation of what the plate portrays. Headings above each printed page recall the relevant cries of agony (or ecstasy) often heard from the touch-line, as accompaniments to the action explained below. The caption at the bottom of each page of comments sums up the main points elaborated on the particular page. As more complicated movements are shown, the explanations become longer—compare those of Part III with Part I. But it is hoped that all through, what the text omits, the photographs will show.

Note. The natural laziness of the authors, added to the inevitable delay encountered in book production over the past few years, which still exists, has spread the making of this book over nearly two years. Hence the hooking technique shown in Plates 53 and 54 is now out-of-date. Under the 1945/6 Law, the hooker alone strikes the ball back, using his far foot. The loose-head player no longer assists him. Nevertheless, the principle of clearing a tunnel through tight scrums remains entirely unaltered.

COACHING COMMENTS

THIS is not a chapter of instruction on coaching : nothing so presumptuous. Every coach has his own methods, be he a Bellower, Grumbler, a Despairer, tho Sarcastic or the Patient Martyr type (see the last plate). And every coach, whatever his methods, has his own interpretation of the game and teaches the game with an emphasis on the aspect of the game which appeals most to himself. All this makes for variety and experiment, which keeps the game interesting and alive—for instance, in International Rugby there is always a distinct contrast between the type of game played by the typical Welsh as opposed to, say, the English XV.

The aim of the ensuing few paragraphs is to introduce ideas in coaching which have occurred to the authors, in the hope that they may help others, be they coaches themselves, players or interested followers of the game.

Coaching in schools must be systematic ; so much of it, one feels, is unco-ordinated without a coach-in-charge, so to speak, to lay down policy. Most schools, it is probably true to say, split boys up into age-groups for Rugger—at the Royal Naval College, Dartmouth, it is under 14, under 15, under 16 and over 16. In such cases, it is worth while, surely, for the senior coach to lay down what he expects the other coaches to cover in each age-group. For example :

Up to 15 . .	Passing, punting and catching, place-kicking, dribbling and falling, low tackling, scrumming and line-out work and correct positioning of Outsides.
Up to 16 revise and add	Kicking with the " worse " foot, drop-kicking, wheeling, detailed and more specific teaching on individual covering and defensive positioning, different tackles, intensive backing-up and short-passing by Forwards, swerving and side-stepping.
Over 16 revise and add	Constructive kicking during a game—e.g. cross-kicking—team moves and simple tactics, individual manœuvres.

Each coach will have his own ideas. Some boys, despite age, will advance quickly in technique and be able to go ahead. But it will repay the trouble to coach to a system, aiming at important, if limited, objectives each year.

Physical training experts are all emphatic on the necessity for slow progression to advanced work. Do we take enough trouble over this in Rugger training ? For, after all, learning to tackle low confidently and accurately is as much a " drill " in its way as learning to vault over a box-horse. As with vaulting, it must be taught in detail and slowly—standing, then on a slow-moving target, and so on. The good player is good—like the efficient fighter—because drill plus instinct make him do the right thing at the right time.

Let us be thorough too. Passing is not everything in Rugger, and a practice is something more than a vague kick-about, followed by passing for Outsides and scrum practice for the Forwards. What of kicking (and don't leave the Full-back to go on kicking till his leg is ready to drop off) and falling, learning to snap up a moving ball off the ground ? Do not leave dribbling practice and instruction to the Forwards only, nor instruction in selling a dummy to the Backs exclusively.

In coaching Outsides, there tends to be a danger of teaching boys to be too long and deliberate in giving a pass. It is probably true to say that, when a boy leaves school and enters Club Rugger, one of his biggest difficulties is not being able to pass quickly enough ; in fact, in nine cases out of ten, he cannot do it for his first season and probably gets into bad habits as a result of it. The fault for much of this may lie with coaches who over-emphasize the long swinging action in passing. Let us admit that the pass is a quick wristy action, with the follow-through as the only deliberate part of it—and that the most important part. Further, many coaches object to seeing boys practise passing when running at half-speed. " Flat out when you pass," they bellow. Why ? Why not go at half-speed if the boys are picking up the timing and balance of giving a pass ? Surely all technique has to be learned in slow time.

Talking of passing, there is no need to bring up Centres in the habit of never giving a Wing a pass, unless it gives him a chance to score. Never mind waiting to give him a scoring chance ; the Wing wants to join in the game, have a dash at his opposite number, get his blood up. Give him the ball, even if only for a six-yard run, for most Wings like the " feel " of the ball and to try a hand-off or swerve. And if things are too hot, the touch-line is near enough. Furthermore, Wings, never worry too much about the return pass inside : concentrate on running, go on running and don't let them stop you !

It is time that coaches and players took more trouble with kicking of all kinds. Touring sides from the Empire are always envied for the length of their kicking, which is probably nothing more than the result of patient practice. As for drop-kicking and efficient place-kicking, it is enough to point out that a dropped goal is worth more than an unconverted try and that two converted tries will beat three unconverted tries. Intelligent practice can produce really reliable kicking, and reliable kicking will produce many points,

For too long, kicking has been a neglected art in this country. Two warnings, however, are necessary on the subject of kicking. First, aimless kicking makes Rugger very dull—particularly continual touch-finding by a fly-half. Second, kicking ahead is a complete waste if it gives the opposition possession. Beware the player who uses the kick ahead (the kick in the direction in which the player is running, as opposed to the frequently desirable cross-kick which changes the direction of the attack). Players should not use the kick ahead unless it is placed well out of reach of the Full-back. A well-placed kick ahead is an admirable move, and particularly if the defence is marking-up and is to be driven back. A bad kick ahead is a gift to the opposition.

Halves, of course, must go on assiduously practising together, experimenting, getting to know each other. Let them and all players " fool about " with the ball a bit during practices, on their own. They learn much that way. First and foremost try to get Halves to be proud of the *speed* of their passing. They, above all, have the power of defeating spoiling Wing-forwards. It is a crime for either Half to be caught with the ball. Incidentally, for the Scrum-half to roll the ball against a goal-post enables him to practise passing out from a very realistic artificial " heel."

When Halves and Three-quarters combine for practice in passing movements, it is surely better to attack the try-line from a 25—the ball to travel across the line twice at the most—rather than to indulge in long straggling movements for the entire length of the field. When a line of Outsides practices these passing movements, they should run slightly diagonally towards a corner flag for, in a game, a line never runs quite straight. Teach the Full-back to join in these movements and, at the same time, the " unemployed " Wing Three-quarter to drop back in the Full-back's place, whenever this occurs.

The importance of positioning all the time in attack and defence must be emphasised and re-emphasised continually. The good player scores tries because he knows how and when to back-up the break-through, and he is hard to beat in defence because he is always in position, covering his opposite number. A simple method of teaching positioning, in attack and defence, for two sets of Out-sides, is to line them up opposite each other and then to kick the ball into any part of the field of play. Where the ball comes to rest represents a scrum-position and the Outsides must be positioned, exactly, by the time the ball comes to rest.

When it comes to manœuvres and team tactics, again these must be taught slowly and clearly. Boys will so rarely try them on in a match because they lack the confidence to do so : and invariably because the move has been taught too briefly and quickly, instead of slowly and almost " by numbers."

In coaching Forwards we should teach them to remember the cardinal rule : " Look what you are doing." So many schoolboys shove " blind " and jump with fright at a quick pass. Perhaps endless scrumming practices deaden the reactions ! And how many Forwards can really picture what an overlap means when a defending Outside is " down " ! How a couple of seconds' delay in heeling from a loose-scrum can give the opposition time to get back into position. If only they would appreciate that. Coaches should keep on dinning in the fact that tries are scored from loose play, and that a quick heel in the loose is worth two from the " tight " or line-out when both sets of Outsides are fully positioned and ready.

Be specific in explaining the duties of all Forwards. True, they work as a pack, but the second row *does* traditionally tend to follow up the middle of the field and the young player may not know that. Nor may the middle of the back row realise that he is expected to mark the Scrum-half when that player steals round on the blind side. Or, alternatively, he may have seen that done and you may disapprove of it, so be specific in instructing the Forwards.

In conclusion, here are three points. Firstly, coaches should emphasise the advantages to be gained from a quick pick up. For instance, a snap pick up and pass after a tackle (play it with your foot first), after a dropped pass or a too strong dribble forward. The Welsh are past-masters in this. It does speed up the game and it does provide some wonderful scoring chances. Secondly, do not overdo the amount of Rugger for schoolboys. It is a very strenuous form of exercise. A match and two practices or two games in a single week should be quite enough. And if they are urging for a game, so much the better ! Thirdly, not too much boosting of the " Wing " forward in defence : of " near-offside " tactics. Much of that spoils Rugger. Many of the beat-the-Referee tactics would be eliminated if they were rudely and actively discouraged in the schoolboy and young Club player, instead of being connived at or accounted a form of self-preservation. It is time that coaches took a stand on this. No amount of amendment to the Rules of Rugby can do half of what coaches and players themselves can do in this. Further, good Club and County sides should not go on playing the player of doubtful habits. In this, representative sides are too often to blame.

Rugger in the next decade will be what the coach and young player of to-day makes it in technique and tactics. The game is worth a thought.

INTRODUCTION TO PART I

THIS explains the simple fundamentals of the game, such as passing, tackling and kicking—technique on which every player's game must be based.

May we make a few comments on what follows in Part I?

Passing. Do not overdo the swing in giving a pass—especially in practising from standing : a short swing is quickly carried on by a wristy push-away. It requires a quick movement in which the only deliberate part is that of the follow-through, combined with the swing away of the hips.

Tackling. Practise this "at the walk," slowly speeding up. So much alleged funking is due to a young player's lack of confidence, arising from lack of ability to carry out the correct drill. Bad falling on the ball is often due to the same cause.

Physical training experts make much of the necessity of carefully taught "progressions" in gymnastic work—in rope climbing or vaulting. In other words, knowledge and confidence are essential in simple drill before more advanced work can be attempted. Do we Rugger coaches always remember that? Passing practice, yes. But how much do we worry about carefully planned practices in tackling, falling and kicking? And for everybody, Backs and Forwards as well.

7

1

2

3

I. Holding the Ball

Hands along the seams, slightly behind the central seam.
Note. With a wet ball the hands should move even further
back behind the central seam.
Fingers pointed downwards, parallel to the seams.

2. Giving a Pass (i)

Feet carry on at top speed in their original direction as the
Body swivels on the
Hips towards the receiver, and the
Arms and Hands are drawn back away from the receiver. Do
not overdo this movement : keep the
Outside Elbow up, and the
Eyes on the man who is to receive the pass.

3. Giving a Pass (ii)

Feet continuing at full speed, allow the
Body to fall into the *opponent* as the ball is passed. To give
the pass the
Hands swing across the body, while the
Wrists and Fingers " push " the ball, to give it speed and
direction, and follow-through after it.
Eyes concentrate on the aiming point—ahead of the receiver,
chest high—to enable him to take the ball with speed
unchecked.
Note particularly Sugden's fingers, hands, head and eyes concentrating on the vital follow-through.

"Top-speed, look and follow-through"

4

5

4. Taking a Pass (i)

Run at top speed, and straight.
Head and shoulders turned, ready.
Arms comfortably prepared,
Eyes on the ball, and as in

5. Taking a Pass (ii)

Run into the ball,
Fold the ball easily into cradle of arms and body.
Note the wide extended fingers.

"Look at the ball and take it at top speed"

6

7

6. The Ordinary Tackle (standing)

Leg drives body at opponent (left leg here) forcing
Shoulder into opponent's thigh, as the
Arms enclose and grip both legs above the knee.
Eyes watch the victim's thighs all the time until the
Head arrives behind the opponent's buttocks.
Note that the head is placed behind the victim, who will other-
    wise fall on his tackler's head—which is as unnecessary a
    process as it is painful!

7. Tackling as Above (action)

The whole process repeated exactly, but the
Leg drive becomes a *dive* and the
Shoulder knocks the opponent over as the
Arms strangle his legs.
Note. Repeat—the victim is not dragged down, in the ideal
    tackle, but literally knocked over by the impact of the
    shoulder.

8

9

10

11

"GET HIM . . ."

8. Front Tackle

Note. This is a " snap " tackle to be used if and when you are caught standing, with an opponent coming straight at you.
Feet and Body to one side of the opponent : let him come into your
Inside Arm and Shoulder. Grip his thighs tight and let his momentum, as he falls, carry you over backwards. Keep your
Head to the " free " side, or the opponent's knees will hit it and his body trap it as he falls.

9. Smother Tackle

Note. The only legitimate high tackle, to be used to stop a man passing at all costs—say, an opponent very close to your line. To avoid a hand-off, the action is fundamentally as in Plate 7, but the
Arms envelop the opponent's arms and the ball, instead of his thighs. The
Head, as usual, out of the way, while the weight and momentum of the tackler should bowl over the opponent.

10, 11. Tackle Positioning

Note. This concerns the Full-back most of all, but in principle, all players. Always edge a man one way : never stand dead ahead of him. When you can—and that is often—edge him down the " tunnel " made by your positioning and the touch-line.
Full-backs—this concerns you more than anyone else ! Here the runner is a left Wing Three-quarter being approached
Correctly in Plate 10—being shepherded into the " tunnel "
—and
Incorrectly in Plate 11, being allowed to swing away from the touch-line and into the middle of the field.

"Look at what you mean to hit and do it hard"

12

13

14

12. Dribbling

Note. Whichever of the two methods used with the feet, as
explained below, keep the
Ball close to the feet and do not try to go too fast, keeping the
Body forward,
Head down all the time with the
Eyes directly over the ball.

13. Dribbling (Inside-of-Foot Method)

Dribble with the inside of the foot, with
Legs splayed wide, generally playing the ball with each foot in
turn. This gives control when the ball is bumping from
side to side.

14. Dribbling (Outside-of-Foot Method)

Legs closer together, using the outside of the foot to impart
back-spin. This keeps the ball close but gives less control
of lateral " play " on the ball. In a skilled dribbler, it
allows for speedier dribbling than the Inside-of-Foot method.
Note. This method is ideal when a player is running on to a
loose ball. Provided that the ball is struck low down, close
to the ground, the resulting back spin will keep the ball
close and bring it under control very quickly.

"Concentrate on the ball and do not try to go
too fast"

15

16

17

"FALL ON IT . . ."

15. Wrong!

Body wrong with face towards the opponent's feet—dangerous obviously ; and the ball has not been collected—it cannot be, for it is actually on the dribbler's foot. This is bad timing and bad positioning.

16. Right Timing of a Fall

Ball has just been played forward by the dribbler's foot, enabling the faller to fall properly :
Back towards the opponent,
Arms ready and
Eyes on the ball.

17. Right Positioning

The Back makes a barrier which upsets the dribbler and enables the faller to collect the ball into his
Arms. His Forwards will soon be round and
Note . . . having fallen and broken up the dribble, the " faller " must *at once* release the ball, get up or roll away : but *not* obstruct by continuing to hold the ball.

" Back to opponent and collect the ball deliberately "

18

19

20

18. Ball Ready for a " Punt "

Ball held straight to front, pointed down, lace on top.
Body faces point to which ball is to be kicked ;
Upper hand ready to place the ball down on to the kicking foot,
while the
Other hand, having positioned the ball, steadies it

19. Ball on the Foot

as the foot comes up with
Toe pointed away, foot straight, ankle flexed, the ball is dropped
direct on to the
Instep, as shown,

20. Kick and Follow-through

and as impact is made with a
Straight Leg, the
Foot follows right up : the
Toe still pointing away. The kicker lifts up on to the
Toe of the standing foot :
Body into the kick :
Eyes ahead, on the ball.
Note. (*a*) When kicking into the wind, and only then, cut down
the follow-through, in order to keep the ball low.
(*b*) Experienced players advance to different technique
to suit themselves, to " screw " the ball into touch, and
so on. These plates simply demonstrate the fundamentals
upon which all " punt " kicking is based.

"Take trouble with the ball, and follow-through
high "

21

22

2

"TRY A DROP . . ."

21. Make Ready for a Drop-kick

Body facing the point to which the ball is to go,
Arms forward and
Hands along the sides of the ball.
Note. The ball must touch the ground in the position as shown in—

22. The Start of the Kick

The Ball has been dropped at the correct angle,
Standing Foot up to the ball,
Body relaxed and steady,
Eyes on the ball.
As a tribute to Barlee's happy knack with a camera, this was not a " still," but an " action " photograph.

23. The Drop-kick

Toe pointed away,
Leg straight on contact with the ball,
Standing Heel raised and
Eyes still watching kicking foot.

24

25

24. Placing the Ball for a Place-kick

(*A*) Make a " clean " hole and be careful to place the ball exactly over it.
The angle which the ball makes with the goal-posts is a matter of taste. But do
(i) make sure that the ball is *not* leaning to one side, and
(ii) make sure that the lace is vertically upright and facing the kicker except when the ball is placed pointing at the posts, in which case the lace should be on the under-side.
(*B*) *Note* the " placer " (traditionally the Scrum-half). He is well down, comfortable and concentrating on the ball.
The *lower hand*, the one nearer the posts, checks position: while the *upper hand* will place the ball down, on the order " Down."

25. Ready to Kick

Do be absolutely sure that the
Kicking foot,
Ball and
Centre of the cross-bar are in an exact straight line. Note the vertical line in the Plate to illustrate this.

26. " Down "

As the kicker advances, ordering " Down," the placer puts the ball *firmly* into the hole, lifting the hands *gently* away from the ball.

Note. The kicker must give the " placer " plenty of time to put the ball down. Don't worry unduly about the charge by the opposition.

27. The Place-kick

The Standing Toe goes well up to the ball, while the

Kicking Foot swings back as the body checks ; and, as with all kicks, the kicking foot must be quite straight on impact and must follow-through as in Plate 20.

Eyes, as always, are on the ball.

"Don't let's go on neglecting this scoring kicking"

28   29   30

31

28, 29. Preparing to Catch

Body under control and balanced.
Arms and Chest ready to make a " cradle,"
Eyes on the ball.

30. Held !

The ball is folded into the " cradle," with
Elbows close in to the body.

31. " Mark ! "

When fielding a kick under pressure, a Mark provides an ideal method of gaining relief.

By making a Mark, a player is entitled to a Free Kick from the point where the Mark was made. Before taking the kick be sure to retire from the Mark so as to have plenty of room to make the run up. To gain a Mark

Stand firm at the instant in which the ball is fielded. As it is held, dig in the

Heel, as shown here, and, to avoid confusion, call " Mark " at the same time.

" Never let it bounce first "

INTRODUCTION TO PART II

THIS part of the book explains more advanced technique : practices which all players, as they improve, will begin to wish to try.

Scrum-half's pass. This is specialist technique pre-eminently. But all players should understand it, for the Scrum-half is often trapped at the bottom of a loose scrum—or he may be off the field, hurt—at which time any other player may be required at once to carry on the Scrum-half's duties.

Hand-off. Teach everyone this simple move. It is so easy, so often practicable and so effective.

Side-step or swerve. Many players grow to do one or the other of these deviations almost automatically. Note your own natural tendency and develop it.

32

33

34

32. Putting the Ball into the Scrum

Stand one yard clear of your "loose-head" side—i.e. on
that side of the scrum where your own front-row man has
the outer berth (see Plate 54).

Hold the ball lengthways, below the knee, and lob it into
the middle of the gap between the front rows and beyond the
outside foot of the players flanking the "hookers."

33. Scrum-half's Normal Pass (i)

Note. The most essential features in this are
(*a*) speed of movement, and (*b*) accuracy of the pass. Put
the ball into the scrum on the "loose-head" side (see
Plate 54), and, on coming round to take it after the heel
(you will be standing there already from a loose-scrum), see
that the

Foot farthest from the Fly-half, the

Hands and the Ball all meet close up to each other to start the
single sweeping movement which will get the ball away.

The Outer Foot stands wide pointing towards the Fly-half.
When the ball is grasped the

Eyes sight the Fly-half's "middle"—but eyes on the ball until
it has been grasped—while the

Shoulders begin the swing towards the outer foot,

34. Scrum-half's Normal Pass (ii)

the movement is taken up by

Arms and Hands which sweep the ball straight off the ground.
To ensure accuracy of the pass, the arms, which remain
straight, and the hands follow-through hard to their full
limit, following the direction of the

Eyes. Only thus will the accuracy and control be acquired to
make a long, flat pass to the Fly-half—the longer and flatter
the better, to enable the Fly-half to stand and keep clear of
the Forwards.

35

36

37

35. Scrum-half's Reverse Pass (i)

Note. This is an alternative method of getting a pass away. Circumstances often force a Scrum-half to screw right round, 180°, to get the ball away. Speed of movement and accuracy of the pass are again the vital factors.

Feet, Hands and Ball for the initial movement are exactly as in Plate 33, except that the body is facing in the opposite direction, the Fly-half being to the left of the scrum as he was for Plate 33.

Eyes again watch the ball as it is grasped and then begin to look for the Fly-half's " middle."

36. Scrum-half's Reverse Pass (ii)

Body weight is transferred across towards the man who is to receive the ball. Again this brings

Shoulders, Arms (straight) and Hands swinging through with the ball.

Eyes and Hands are co-ordinated at the end of the movement to give speed and direction and the final follow-through, which finally makes or mars the pass. Study this Plate carefully.

37. The Fly-half taking the Pass

This Plate gives a clear illustration of how a Scrum-half, by passing ahead of his Fly-half, enables the latter and his Three-quarters to get well off the mark, i.e. as the ball is coming well ahead of him, the Fly-half *must* move quickly if he is to reach it in time.

" Get the feet right and 'sweep' the ball away "

38

39

38, 39. Hand-off High and Low

First always move the ball to the " free " side. Hand-off with the open palm, thrusting the tackler firmly away, at the same time using the resistance of the tackler to carry the body away from him (Plate 39).

Note. This " push away " will be most effective when the weight of the body is on the leg nearest the tackler (Plate 39). The high hand-off (Plate 38) necessitates an upward push to the chin ; the low hand-off (Plate 39) a downward thrust against the back of the head.

"Hand-off firmly and deliberately"

40

41

42

This is a simple method of beating a man by feinting to pass, which puts the defender off his balance, enabling the giver of the dummy to pass the defender as he goes for the second man.

40, 41. The Action of the Dummy

The whole
Action of the Pass is carried out, including the deliberate process of turning
Body, Head and Eyes. Make the
follow-through as well emphasised as possible (Plate 40). This action should convince both the defender *and* your partner that a pass is really intended. At the
Last moment of the pass
Pull the ball into the body as you
Change direction suddenly, moving
Away from your partner. If you have sold the dummy convincingly, this will take you clean past your opponent, whose weight will be concentrated on moving towards your partner.
Note. As always when you have beaten your man, cut back towards your " strength," i.e. the bulk of your own players.

42. The Timing of the Dummy

Give your dummy a fair distance before reaching your opponent, in order to give yourself room to change direction wide of him ; otherwise, if you move too close to him, he may recover to grab you at the last moment as you pass him.
Note. In contrast to the remark at the top of the page that the dummy is a simple manœuvre, it must be pointed out that the best dummy is one which is done spontaneously and instantaneously. It cannot be a long premeditated move. Both to " seller " and " taker," a pass must be anticipated and expected right up till the instant shown in Plate 40.

" Be convincing with your eyes and head "

43   44

45   46

A player with the ball should always be able to beat one man. He will almost certainly either swerve or side-step, naturally. Whichever you do, automatically, work it up and improve it.

43, 44. The Side-step

Drive off the
Foot away from the side to which you intend to move, using the
Inside of the Foot, while the
Other Foot is carried sideways. The
Weight of the Body moves over to this latter foot as it lands. Take the weight of the body on the
Outside of this Foot as the foot drives sideways again. Next, the original foot provides the drive so that a series of sideway " jabs " take place, in which the feet keep close but *never* cross.

45, 46. The Swerve

The Hips start the movement by a quick swing in the intended direction of the swerve, the weight being taken on the
Standing Leg (on the swerve side), while the
Outside Leg crosses over to carry the body in its new direction.
Note. (*a*) Begin to swerve well short of your opponent. A side-step starts later. (*b*) Experience will enable you to counter the initial swing-away of the hip by a movement of the head and shoulders in the opposite direction which will automatically increase the emphasis of the cross-over action of the leg, and will help further to baffle your opponent. (*c*) Hold the ball on the swerve side, which will leave the inside hand clear to hand off.

"Drive hard off the feet and ankles"

47   48

49

Use this kick (*a*) when hemmed in—a Wing Three-quarter often is, or (*b*) as a Fly-half or Centre Three-quarter to drive back opponents who are marking-up. But the kick is no more than a wilful method of giving the opposition possession, unless it is skilfully placed well away from the Full-back and other opponents. This is too seldom realised.

47, 48, 49. The Kick Ahead

Note. This is a controlled kick, depending on accuracy, not distance. The key to success is to kick the ball in an upright position, so that it will fall end-over-end and so in landing, " sit up " or roll on straight forward. Therefore, according to inclination and experience, *flick* the ball up off either a

Low Foot (*Plate* 48) *or High Foot* (*Plate* 47), ensuring that the instep hits the

Ball low down while it is in the upright position.

The Toe is bent back to check distance, while in the High Foot position the knee is bent.

Eyes watch the ball on to the foot.

See Plate 49 for an idea of the height required.

" Flick the ball : do not kick it "

50

51

" PICK IT UP . . . "

So often a quick pick-up will clear a difficult position in defence, and in attack set a side moving again.   Often there is time for a deliberate pick-up, but on other occasions a quick " save " is vital—say when a Three-quarter falls back to collect a kick which has dropped behind him.

50. Picking Up (i)

Note. The secret of both methods is to get the
Foot,
Hands and Ball close up together in the action of picking up, with the
Eyes glued on the ball.
In this method get the
Outside of the Foot close to the ball and with
Bent Knee and Body stretch the
Arms to pick up the ball, moving all the time.
(As a matter of interest, Barlee took this apparent " still " when Hollis was moving at top speed.)

51. Picking Up (ii): Alternative Method

Exactly as above, but to get the ball to the
Inside of the Foot while on the move, a hopping pace is required as the runner reaches the ball—just as the hop-step in throwing a cricket ball.

" Get your foot close and watch the ball "

26

INTRODUCTION TO PART III

THE last part of the book deals with Rugger from the team point of view. Part I was fundamental technique ; Part II, still dealing with the individual, passed on to slightly more advanced practices ; Part III leaves the individual and deals with combined team-work : Forwards first, Outsides second.

The key to what is shown in this part is " correct drill." Do let players be clear about their duties at all times. Like fighting, much of the secret of successful Rugger lies in the intelligent application of drill.

We have finished this Part with the Scissors. It is a team move, like the Cross-kick, for it requires the co-operation of a second player. And, with the Cross-kick, the " coming-in " of Wing Three-quarter or Full-back and the Dummy, it seems to be a manœuvre which is well within the compass of the more experienced young player.

5

"SCRUM HERE . . ."

These photographs show, at once, how to pack in a tight-scrum and the tunnel through which the ball should pass when heeled.

52. Binding

Arms comfortably interlocked and gripping tight. The " hooker " should grasp the

Muscle which forms the dorsal edge of the arm-pits of the outside men. Here he has gone too low. The outside men grip the hooker round the

Waist.

Note. It is always better for the hooker to use the over-grip as in this Plate, for it (*a*) drives his head and shoulders into the opposing scrum as a wedge, and (*b*) it puts him well on top of the centre-line of the tunnel between the front rows, for hooking.

53. Front Row (at best, stocky, strong-shouldered men, well matched for size)

For the binding, note that the

Outside players' outside feet are forward while they shove off the

Inside of the rear foot. (This outside-foot-up is the normal method, although an alternative method is for the outside men to put the outside foot back, and so to shove off that foot.)

Hips close,

Backs straight (keeping the heads back will help in this),

Shoulders level, tight close together,

Outside Arms on the shoulders of the opposing front row,

Eyes looking for the ball, which, in this Plate having been put in on the right, is about to be hooked and projected into the tunnel.

Note. The most important task of the front row, in packing, is to be absolutely tight and solid with the shoulders.

54

" HOOKING "

54.

*The action of hooking is a combined movement by the hooker and the man on the side on which the ball has entered.

Note. In all succeeding photographs, the arrow shows the course of the ball as it is heeled back. The

Ball is put in on the

Loose-head side of the scrum. The

Hooker " strikes " the ball back with the

*Far Foot while the

Outside Foot of the Loose-head Player swings in after the ball, projecting it into the tunnel.

Note. (i) Plate 54 shows the loose-head clearly and the hooker using his further foot with which to hook.

(ii) The position of the Loose-head's rear foot is bad (incidentally, it is hard to show a good position while hooking without the pressure of the second and third rows), and the hooker has lost the grip of his outside arm altogether.

(iii) The hand of the White hooker is gripping well—right of Plate.

* Under the 1945/6 Rule that the hooker alone strikes the ball back, the loose-head player, forced to remain inactive until the hooker's far foot has played the ball, is no longer able to co-operate in the hooking process as shown in Plates 53 and 54.

55. The Second Row (the big men)

The ball continues along the tunnel made by the positioning of the feet of the second row. Again, the shove is largely off the

Side of the Rear Foot from which, as the " shove " is given on the entry of the ball into the scrum, comes the drive forward.

The Hips must be close and level, in order to make a solid " target " for the middle of the third row. The

Backs straight, with the

Shoulders low up under the buttocks of the front-row men,

Outside Arms round the front row's buttocks, but *not* impeding their leg movement.

Eyes really watch for the ball.

Note. (*a*) The tendency of the direction of the second-row shove is inwards on to the hooker : most important.

(*b*) To have a clear tunnel for the heeling of the ball, common sense dictates that the second-row men must agree to place their

Inside Feet up (as shown here) or back. Each *must* do the same, for this alone enables the middle-man of the back row to transmit a straight push.

(*c*) The right-hand man's " seat " is a shade too high.

(*d*) The position of that loose hand over the hooker's back is very bad.

56. The Back Row (fast men, with a big man in the middle)

The centre man binds on the second row,

Feet level and wide-placed to leave the tunnel clear. The outside men place the

Inside Arm loosely on the middle man, shoving off the

Outside Foot against the outside buttock of the second row, and shoving in towards the hooker.

Note. For the members of the third row, the action and position of shoving is as for the other members of the pack, except that, as stated, they do not bind closely together, and there is no need to keep the hips close together.

"Pack fiercely, make solid binding No. I priority and shove together"

57

58

"WHEEL, AND TAKE IT . . ."

The wheel is generally a defensive move, aimed at taking the ball away during a heel. As a defensive move, the wheel should always swing towards the touch-line and thus away from the bulk of the attacking side. It requires " pack-work " and must be carried out rapidly and unexpectedly but, done effectively, is most difficult to stop.

57. Wheeling (i)

The ball is heeled normally, then held by the

Second or Third Row as the heeling pack swings towards the touch-line. (See this Plate, the ball marked with an arrow.)

The Front Row remain down as long as possible to swing and bind the opposing scrum. Of the front-row men, the man away from the wheel must give way to allow the hooker to pivot as the man on the inside of the wheel advances, swinging towards his hooker.

The Back Row really start the wheel and remain down and bind on to the second row until the ball is clear, so that the wheeling unit remains a compact body ; but once the ball is clear, up must come the

Heads as the dribble starts.

Note. These Plates show the ball being held by the second rather than the third row, for it is felt that this gives greater bulk to the wheeling unit. On the other hand, it is as common for the back row to do the holding of the ball, followed by the breakaway. This puts the wheeling unit further away from the opposition, the back row can break quicker and more easily than the second and can move more freely ; and, if the wheel is failing, they can quickly heel to the Scrum-half.

58. Wheeling (ii)

The ball is taken wide towards the touch-line—to get it away from the opposing pack. As the

Second Row come clear, they stand up to start an orthodox dribble, supported by the back row, the

Front Row remaining down until the opposing front row breaks up, when they must join the remainder of the wheeling Forwards, coming in on the inside of the wheel.

Note. To Counter a Wheel, the inside back-row man of the opposition scrum—marked X—must come *straight up and,* followed by his pack, immediately, and before the wheeling pack get their heads up, must " bore in " to become the first man of a counter-scrum against the wheeling unit.

"Get a good swing on, and wheel wide"

59

60

61

Ball
×

Back Forward
of Line-Out'

Fly-ha

Do not wait with your arms raised before the ball is thrown in, but have them at shoulder level, ready.

59. The Line-out (i)

Jump if and as the ball comes within reach, using every inch of your height. If the ball is clearly not coming to you,
Form round the man with the ball, getting behind him as quickly as possible, and spotting the whereabouts of the ball, at once.

60. The Line-out (ii)

As you catch the ball and land, generally speaking it is advisable to
Turn towards your opponents, placing the
Ball at your
Feet, or begin to go through holding the ball, preparatory to starting a dribble. In either case,
The Rest of the Pack must be behind
Binding in a loose-scrum for a heel : or adding weight and close support if the ball is being " taken away " in a dribble.
Note. Congregating closely like this will compel the opposing pack to do the same and so leave your Halves free from interference.

61. Passing Back

Passing back is a very different thing from patting back. Patting the ball back is inaccurate and, therefore, wasteful and dangerous. Never do it !
Pass back only if you are free to give the ball to the Scrum-half directly, and quickly enough to ensure that he will not be caught in possession. Opportunities for doing this are rare against good marking. To be successful, the ball must be caught and passed back in almost a single motion.
Note. Whereas the average Forward rarely has the opportunity of passing back directly, when *the rear man* in a line-out obtains the ball, he will generally be able to pass the ball back. As in this Plate, let it go direct to the Fly-half, when passed from the extreme rear of a line-out.

"Possession is worthless without close support from the rest of the pack"

"TAKE IT AWAY, FORWARDS . . ."

There are two cardinal rules to be observed when Forwards start either inter-passing or dribbling, namely (*a*) keep close and (*b*) keep the man with the ball in the middle of the pack.

62, 63. Inter-passing

Plate 62 is *Wrong !*

Wrong because the man holding the ball is on a flank, and so unsupported and unprotected on one side ; thus he can pass the ball only to his left if an opponent threatens him. Plate 63 is *Right !*

64

Right because the player with the ball is well supported on both flanks and so able to pass the ball to another of his own side, either to the left or right.

Note. The player on the left of the man with the ball has run in front of the ball. Remember, in such movements, to keep behind the man with the ball, otherwise he cannot pass to you.

64, 65. Forwards Dribbling

As for 62 for passing, so Plate 64 is
Wrong and for exactly the same reasons. The man in possession must be supported on each flank as in Plate 65. Plate 65 is *Right !*
Right because the dribbler, if threatened by an opponent, can slip the ball to the player on either side of him.

" Keep close and cover both flanks "

65

E*

"BACK UP . . ."

66.

This is a shot of the England-Scotland Match of 1934, at Twickenham, reproduced, as with Plates 67 and 75, with acknowledgements to *The Times*.

The photograph shows how widely the England Forwards (marked F, in white) have dispersed in attack. They are wide, to cover every possible change in the direction of the attack, backing up along the touch-line, and yet covering the middle of the field—ready, particularly, for a cross-kick, which is the especial duty of the

Second Row.

The faster forwards (usually the

Back Row) should back up the Outsides actually in possession, while the remainder use intelligent anticipation in getting ready for the attack to swing back towards the centre again as it is beginning to in this Plate.

"Use your head and position yourself intelligently"

67. Forwards in Defence

This is the Rugby-Uppingham Match of 1936.

It provides a very clear illustration of the look of the pack in defence. Namely, to cover up behind the Outsides, aiming diagonally (see the arrow) across the field in order to cut off a break-through. Here the White Forwards seem to be moving rather slowly.

When the ball is got away by the opposition, there *is* a chance for quick-breaking Forwards to kill the attack by quick tackling of the Halves. Generally speaking, however, the ball should be got away by the side in possession, which necessitates covering by the whole of the pack. In this Plate the bulk of the defending Forwards, Rugby in White, are having to " corner flag."

"Cover well back, and move fast"

"A MAN OVER . . ."

68. The " Overlap "

Coaches are always urging a quick heel in the loose when attacking. Why ? Because a

Quick Loose Heel following a tackle will often give the attacking Outsides the ball, while an opposing Outside is still on the ground with his colleagues possibly out of position too.

This is the attacking Three-quarter's dream, for a quick passing movement to the Wing will find the Wing

Over-lapping the defence.

This Plate shows a Blue attack, using an exaggerated overlap with the White defence a man short—on the ground inside the scrum (left)—and the remainder out of position.

Such is the scoring chance Outsides may be missing by slow heeling, which gives the defence time to re-form.

Halves and Centres Beware ! Recognise an overlap when it occurs and " whisk " the ball straight out to the Wing. To attempt to cut through on your own is thoroughly bad play in such a case.

69. Making the Extra Man

Let Wing Three-quarters or Full-backs, from scrums near the line or at an opponents' throw-in, come up to make this precious overlap.

Here the Wing has come in to take the pass from the Scrum-half and send the ball straight on. Alternatively he, or the Full-back, could have come in between the Centres.

Note. Be ready for the opposition to attempt this when they, in turn, are attacking. Wings, particularly, beware !

"Prepare your plan quickly, pass quickly and you're away !"

70

71

70. Outsides in Attack (i)

Wrong !

Wrong because the line is lying flat, so that all have to move up slowly for fear of over-running the ball. No one will be able to take the ball at speed—and imagine how obligingly close they must be to the opposition line.

Note. The left Centre is particularly to blame for, more than any, his position has spoiled the line.

71. Outsides in Attack (ii)

Right !

Right because by positioning deep, the Fly-half and his colleagues are enabled to take the ball at top speed. The *Halves* have started them off right, so that the Centres and Wing must stride out if they are to keep up at all.

Further, by standing deep the Blues have increased the distance between themselves and the opposing line, thus providing themselves with more vital manœuvring room.

"Lie deep and be quick off your mark"

Fly-half
and both Centres

72

73

72. Outsides in Defence (i)

Wrong !

Wrong because the Blues are advancing unevenly, leaving gaps such as that between the right Centre and the right Wing in the foreground. They are simply advancing according to individual whim.

73. Outsides in Defence (ii)

Right !

Right because the Blues are advancing successively and evenly as a unit, driving the opposition outwards and at an angle away from the pack.

This technique leaves a minimum of " gaps " and enables the defence to " direct " the attack to the touch-line, rather than to allow the attack room for initiative.

Note. (i) Whereas the scheme of defence is to " run " the attack into touch, it is often a paying tactic to turn the Fly-half (and him only) " inside " to be " killed " by the pack and cut off from his Centres.

(ii) Once his opposite number has got rid of the ball, the tendency of the Outside in defence should be, like the pack, to " corner-flag," to " cover-up " his colleagues.

"Move up wisely, and cover each other"

74. The Cross-kick

The cross-kick is simply a method of transferring the ball, in attack, to a single player or group of unmarked members of the side who are out of passing range. The kick may be short or long and is an ideal move for a hemmed-in Wing Three-quarter or other players under such pressure.

The kick is a

Diagonal kick, requiring the orthodox kicking technique, but let the

Ball point in its intended direction as it is dropped on to the

Foot which must, obviously, hook the ball.

To be effective, the ball must pitch well ahead of those for whom it is intended, so as to be *behind* the defence, who can be beaten for possession, by quick following up, as they turn. Therefore, kick deepish—rarely less than 45°, unless you are well up to the opponents' line, in which case drop it just *under* (not behind) the posts and run straight ahead in order to put your colleagues " on side."

75.

England should have scored (and maybe did) by orthodox passing, from the phase shown here, but to illustrate why and when to cross-kick, study this Plate. Imagine the man now being tackled to have kicked from A a fraction earlier, putting the ball in the area of B—a try, surely ? It *is* simple and it *is* effective.

" Kick deep and high "

76

77

76, 77. The " Scissors " (i)

This is not a difficult move and a Rugger player who is being crowded in can often thus change direction and run clear of trouble, for instance, a Wing Three-quarter being crowded into touch. In addition, done discreetly and quickly, it is an ideal pre-conceived plan for misleading the opposition.

As the player to
Receive the ball quickly
Changes direction, the
Passer turns his head to watch receiver, who runs
Close up to the passer. The
Pass is gentle, almost hand to hand, and may be given in the normal way (Plate 77) or by means of a Reverse pass (Plate 76).

If anything, the Reverse pass method is the less conspicuous, though dangerous unless the passer turns his head and eyes to watch the delivery of the pass.

78. The " Scissors " (ii)

This demonstrates the complete change in the direction of the attack and how the receiver must run away from the passer at a wide angle. This he must do unless he is to run straight into the defending Forwards as they cover-up.

" Watch, get close for the pass and open the scissors wide "

COACHES, BEWARE !

DESPAIRER   PATIENT MARTYR   BELLOWER   GRUMBLER

79

79.

Wrong ! *Wrong* because it is bad for your temper, no help to the team, and irritating for your fellow spectators.

"It is but a GAME. Why Worry?"

IN RETROSPECT . . .

THE New Zealand Army Touring XV has visited Britain while this book has been in the making, has won many spectacular successes and left us pondering on the secret of their play. A brief commentary on their methods may serve to emphasise certain aspects of the game, and to illustrate further some of our earlier conclusions.

First, Rugger is a hard game and it is essentially a team game. The Kiwis always stated, to use their particular idiom, that a man who could not stand up to the hard knocks should " stay on the bank." And fundamentally it was team-work which encompassed the fall of British teams which, on paper, could have expected to have defeated the Tourists.

The paramount necessity for quick heeling, acknowledged in theory, but too rarely in practice, by many a team and all coaches, was a positive " No. 1 Priority " with the Kiwis. The entire pack understood perfectly the necessity for possession, and quick possession, and tore into every scrum and line-out with the fixed intention of getting the ball and of sparing no effort to do so. Further than this, the Kiwis understood that after a tackle or dropped pass, to have a man up to play the ball, by heeling it, so that a second man might pick up and start a passing movement, was the way to save time and to catch the defence out of position : no slow forming of a scrum as Forwards arrived, in turn. . . .

The Kiwi Forwards never let up : obsessed with the idea of possession, they implemented this by intensive backing-up, once the ball had reached the Outsides. Again they made effective practice of a generally (and so vaguely) accepted theory—back up. When they backed up, the Kiwi Forwards were intelligently positioned, well up and ready. Whoever saw one surprised to receive a pass ? And in contrast, how few of our School and Club Forwards are really prepared for passes and constructive and accurate in making ground and handing on the ball ?

Quick service and correct positioning, together with clear thinking, produced the accurately and apparently unhurried passing of the Kiwi Backs. Unless there was a chance of a clear break-through, the " centre triangle " passed the ball straight to the Wings. There was neither hesitation nor vague battering against the defence for non-existent openings. Complementary to this feeding of the Wings went accurate return passing back to the Centres or cross-kicks, by the Wings—movements productive of many a try under the posts.

43

Two points require comment. First, there is nothing mysterious about the Five-eighth position. The Five-eighth player is the Centre who, instead of remaining Right or Left Centre, always plays alongside the Fly-half as " first " Centre, so to speak. He is thus known as Five-eighth as the link between the Halves and the one Centre Three-quarter. Second, the Kiwis did not dispense with " close " Forward tactics on principle—wheeling, dribbling rushes, etc. They omitted them by design because the Forwards were light and inexperienced. Such tactics remain as much a necessary part of the game as ever. There is no effective alternative on wet and heavy pitches. On their own admitting the Kiwis always hoped for (and generally found !) dry pitches, because of their weakness in this department.

Let us sum up, then. The Kiwis taught us once again : be fit, go hard, play together, counting on possession of the ball as nine-tenths of the art of the game. Add to this determined tackling and speed to exploit opponents' mistakes and Rugger becomes open, fast, coherent—a great game to play and a spectacular one to watch.